LGBT FAMILIES

Families Today

Adoptive Families

Disability and Families

Foster Families

Homelessness and Families

Immigrant Families

Incarceration and Families

LGBT Families

Military Families

Multigenerational Families

Multiracial Families

Single-Parent Families

Teen Parents

Families Today

LGBT FAMILIES
LESBIAN, GAY, BISEXUAL, AND TRANSGENDER

H.W. Poole

MASON CREST

Mason Crest
450 Parkway Drive, Suite D
Broomall, PA 19008
www.masoncrest.com

MTM Publishing, Inc.
435 West 23rd Street, #8C
New York, NY 10011
www.mtmpublishing.com

President: Valerie Tomaselli
Vice President, Book Development: Hilary Poole
Designer: Annemarie Redmond
Copyeditor: Peter Jaskowiak
Editorial Assistant: Andrea St. Aubin

Series ISBN: 978-1-4222-3612-3
Hardback ISBN: 978-1-4222-3619-2
E-Book ISBN: 978-1-4222-8263-2

Library of Congress Cataloging-in-Publication Data
Names: Poole, Hilary W., author.
Title: LGBT families / by H.W. Poole.
Description: Broomall, PA : Mason Crest [2017] | Series: Families Today | Includes index.
Identifiers: LCCN 2016004545| ISBN 9781422236192 (hardback) | ISBN 9781422236123
(series) | ISBN 9781422282632 (e-book)
Subjects: LCSH: Sexual minorities—Family relationships—Juvenile literature. | Sexual
minority parents—Juvenile literature. | Children of sexual minority parents—Juvenile
literature. | Gay parents—Juvenile literature. | Children of gay parents—Juvenile
literature. | Families—Juvenile literature.
Classification: LCC HQ73 .P66 2017 | DDC 306.874086/6—dc23
LC record available at http://lccn.loc.gov/2016004545

Printed and bound in the United States of America.

First printing
9 8 7 6 5 4 3 2 1

TABLE OF CONTENTS

Key Icons to Look for:

Words to Understand: These words with their easy-to-understand definitions will increase the reader's understanding of the text, while building vocabulary skills.

Sidebars: This boxed material within the main text allows readers to build knowledge, gain insights, explore possibilities, and broaden their perspectives by weaving together additional information to provide realistic and holistic perspectives.

Research Projects: Readers are pointed toward areas of further inquiry connected to each chapter. Suggestions are provided for projects that encourage deeper research and analysis.

Text-Dependent Questions: These questions send the reader back to the text for more careful attention to the evidence presented there.

Series Glossary of Key Terms: This back-of-the-book glossary contains terminology used throughout the series. Words found here increase the reader's ability to read and comprehend higher-level books and articles in this field.

In the 21st century, families are more diverse than ever before.

SERIES INTRODUCTION

Our vision of "the traditional family" is not nearly as time-honored as one might think. The standard of a mom, a dad, and a couple of kids in a nice house with a white-picket fence is a relic of the 1950s—the heart of the baby boom era. The tumult of the Great Depression followed by a global war caused many Americans to long for safety and predictability—whether such stability was real or not. A newborn mass media was more than happy to serve up this image, in the form of TV shows like *Leave It To Beaver* and *The Adventures of Ozzie and Harriet*. Interestingly, even back in the "glory days" of the traditional family, things were never as simple as they seemed. For example, a number of the classic "traditional" family shows—such as *The Andy Griffith Show, My Three Sons,* and a bit later, *The Courtship of Eddie's Father*—were actually focused on single-parent families.

Sure enough, by the 1960s our image of the "perfect family" was already beginning to fray at the seams. The women's movement, the gay rights movement, and—perhaps more than any single factor—the advent of "no fault" divorce meant that the illusion of the Cleaver family would become harder and harder to maintain. By the early 21st century, only about 7 percent of all family households were traditional—defined as a married couple with children where *only* the father works outside the home.

As the number of these traditional families has declined, "nontraditional" arrangements have increased. There are more single parents, more gay and lesbian parents, and more grandparents raising grandchildren than ever before. Multiracial families—created either through interracial relationships or adoption—are also increasing. Meanwhile, the transition to an all-volunteer military force has meant that there are more kids growing up in military families than there were in the past. Each of these topics is treated in a separate volume in this set.

While some commentators bemoan the decline of the traditional family, others argue that, overall, the recognition of new family arrangements has brought more good than bad. After all, if very few people live like the Cleavers anyway, isn't it better to be honest about that fact? Surely, holding up the traditional family as an ideal to which all should aspire only serves to stigmatize kids whose lives differ from that standard. After all, no children can be held responsible for whatever family they find themselves in; all they can do is grow up as best they can. These books take the position that every family—no matter what it looks like—has the potential to be a successful family.

That being said, challenges and difficulties arise in every family, and nontraditional ones are no exception. For example, single parents tend to be less well off financially than married parents are, and this has long-term impacts on their children. Meanwhile, teenagers who become parents tend to let their educations suffer, which damages their income potential and career possibilities, as well as risking the future educational attainment of their babies. There are some 400,000 children in the foster care system at any given time. We know that the uncertainty of foster care creates real challenges when it comes to both education and emotional health.

Furthermore, some types of "nontraditional" families are ones we wish did not have to exist at all. For example, an estimated 1.6 million children experience homelessness at some point in their lives. At least 40 percent of homeless kids are lesbian, gay, bisexual, or transgender teens who were turned out of their homes because of their orientation. Meanwhile, the United States incarcerates more people than any other nation in the world—about 2.7 million kids (1 in 28) have an incarcerated parent. It would be absurd to pretend that such situations are not extremely stressful and, often, detrimental to kids who have to survive them.

The goal of this set, then, is twofold. First, we've tried to describe the history and shape of various nontraditional families in such a way that kids who aren't familiar with them will be able to not only understand, but empathize. We also present demographic information that may be useful for students who are dipping their toes into introductory sociology concepts.

Second, we have tried to speak specifically to the young people who are living in these nontraditional families. The series strives to address these kids as

Meeting challenges and overcoming them together can make families stronger.

sympathetically and supportively as possible. The volumes look at some of the typical problems that kids in these situations face, and where appropriate, they offer advice and tips for how these kids might get along better in whatever situation confronts them.

Obviously, no single book—whether on disability, the military, divorce, or some other topic—can hope to answer every question or address every problem. To that end, a "Further Reading" section at the back of each book attempts to offer some places to look next. We have also listed appropriate crisis hotlines, for anyone with a need more immediate than can be addressed by a library.

Whether your students have a project to complete or a problem to solve, we hope they will be able to find clear, empathic information about nontraditional families in these pages.

—H. W. Poole

Today, pink is viewed as a color for girls and blue for boys, but it has not always been that way.

Chapter One

WHAT DOES LGBT MEAN?

In 1918, an article was published in a magazine for people who sell clothing. The article said, "The generally accepted rule is pink for the boys and blue for the girls. The reason is that pink, being a . . . stronger color, is more suitable for the boy, while blue, which more delicate and dainty, is prettier for the girl."

No, you didn't read that wrong. Just a hundred years ago, people had a totally opposite idea about which colors were "suitable" for girls and boys. What's

Words to Understand

chromosomes: parts of cells that carry genetic information.

discrimination: singling out a group for unfair treatment.

fluid: something that is able to change.

inclusive: broad, accepting of everyone.

orientation: the direction of a person's interests or beliefs.

sibling: brother or sister.

stereotypes: simplified ideas about types of people, rather than actual people.

more, *all* little kids wore dresses back then, not just girls. It had nothing to do with whether the baby was male or female—it was just easier to change their diapers!

Today, girls get pink blankets, while boys get blue. Girl babies wear pajamas in soft colors with flowers or kittens on them, while boys' pajamas have bold stripes decorated with trucks and trains. This is sometimes called "gender coding," and it continues throughout childhood. You can see gender coding in the toys kids play with, the stories they read, and the clothes they wear.

Parents have a lot of ideas about who their babies will become. Daughters are usually expected to be thoughtful and emotional, while sons are expected to be more physical and not let their feelings show. Many parents expect their daughter to grow up, fall in love with and marry a man, and then become a mother herself. They expect their son to grow up, fall in love with and marry a woman, and become a father.

Times are changing, of course. These **stereotypes** are not as powerful as they used to be. But the core beliefs are still there. We tell ourselves: girls act like *this*, boys act like *that*. However, as the quote above shows, our ideas about what's "for boys" and what's "for girls" can change.

UNDERSTANDING IDENTITY

In order to understand what the acronym LGBT is all about, you first have to understand a few terms: sex, gender, and **orientation**.

People often use the words *sex* and *gender* to mean the same thing, but they actually aren't the same. Here, the word *sex* refers to biology; it describes, in a very concrete way, the male or female features of human bodies. On the other hand, *gender* is less concrete. It refers to our ideas about what it means to be a boy or a girl. There are two terms related to gender: *gender identity* is how people see themselves, and *gender expression* is how people dress and how they behave. In other words, do you think of yourself as male or female? That's your gender

Stereotypes about how girls and boys "should" behave or play are changing.

identity. Do you dress and act in a way that makes others see you as male or as female? That's your gender expression.

The last term on our list is *sexual orientation*. That just means what type of person is attractive to you in a romantic way. Now, you yourself may not be interested in anybody in "that way" at the moment. That's totally fine! But chances are, sometime in the next few years, some cute person is going to catch your eye. Who you choose will be influenced by your orientation.

As you can see, these terms all describe very different things. But it can be easy to forget that the terms are different. That's because, for a lot of people, all the terms overlap. In other words, their sex matches up with their gender, and their orientation is what's traditionally expected of that sex.

A person's orientation involves who that person is attracted to.

Let's say there's a person in your class named Emma. When Emma was born, the doctor said, "It's a girl!" These days, Emma likes to wear dresses, write in her diary, and watch the movie *Frozen* over and over. Emma's biological sex is female, and it matches up with both her gender identity and expression.

Then there's another person in your class named Bill. When Bill was born, the midwife said, "It's a boy!" Now Bill plays a lot of football and never ties his sneakers. Like Emma, Bill's sex also matches his gender.

When they get to high school, Emma and Bill go to the prom together. They are both "straight," meaning that Emma is attracted to boys and Bill is attracted to girls. That's their orientation.

This is all great! It's how life works out much of the time. But there are lots of people who don't fit into the Emma-and-Bill mold.

Let's imagine that Bill has a **sibling** named Matt. Unlike Bill, Matt doesn't like sports at all. In fact, Matt doesn't like most of the things boys are "supposed to" like. At school, when the teacher tells the boys to get into one line and the girls into another, Matt isn't totally sure where to stand. Of course, Matt knows that the "right" answer is the boys' line, but that's not what feels right inside.

It's possible that Matt is transgender. That would mean Matt's sex and gender identity are not the same. Of course, it's also possible that Matt is what's called *gender **fluid***, meaning that Matt may never fit perfectly into either the boy or the girl role. Matt also might just be a boy who's just a bit different from other boys. There's no right answer, and Matt doesn't need to figure this all out right away. Sometimes it takes years for people to totally understand their gender identities.

BEING LGBT

In the acronym LGBT, the L and the G stand for *lesbian* and *gay*. Lesbians are women who are romantically attracted to other women. Gay men are romantically attracted to other men. (The word *gay* can also be used to refer to both groups—as in the phrase, "the gay community.")

The B in LGBT stands for *bisexual*, which describes people who can be romantically attracted to both men and women. It's important to understand that bisexual people are not attracted to *every* man and woman they meet! Lots of bisexual people choose one partner and stay with that person. The word *bisexual* simply means that the person can and does feel attractions to either gender.

The final letter in LGBT stands for *transgender*. While the L, G, and B relate to orientation—whoever a particular person wants to date—*transgender* relates to a person's gender. Transgender people's sex at birth (their biology) does not match up with their identity (internal feeling) or expression (external behavior). Transgender people often "transition," which means they live as the gender that

Expanding the Acronym

The acronym *LGBT* covers a large group of people. But sometimes additional letters are added to make the acronym even more **inclusive**. For example, the acronym LGBTQ is becoming more popular: the Q can stand for *questioning*, meaning people who are wondering about their orientation but aren't sure about it. The Q can also stand for *queer*. The term *queer* is sometimes used as an insult, but it also can be a catch-all term for people with any "nontraditional" views on gender. Sometimes people add both Q's, so that the acronym becomes LGBTQQ.

The letter I, short for *intersex*, is also sometimes added. Earlier we noted that the word *sex* refers to a person's biological sex. In the majority of humans, boys have **chromosomes** that we call XY, while girls have XX. But while that is the usual situation, it is not the only one. People can be born with XXY chromosomes, for example. The prefix *inter-* can mean either "between" or "together." Intersex people are those who can't easily be classified as biologically male or female. Some intersex people view themselves as transgender, but many don't. That's why sometimes you'll see the I added, and the acronym becomes LGBTQI.

Sometimes people add A, for *ally* (or friend) of the LGBT community. The A can mean *asexual,* which is a term for people who do not feel romantically attracted to anyone. The acronym starts to look like this: LGBTQQIAA.

Another way people deal with this issue of inclusion is to say LGBT+, with the plus standing for any and all of the different identities that might be included under the LGBT umbrella.

Laverne Cox is a transgender actress who stars in the TV show *Orange is the New Black*.

matches their identity. Some transgender people take medication or have surgery so that their bodies match that identity. But it's not required that they do. There are lots of transgender people who don't have surgery.

WHO MAKES UP AN LGBT FAMILY?

Everybody has parents. Most of us have siblings, cousins, aunts and uncles, and grandparents. We may know these people well, or we may not know them not at all. But the point is that everybody comes from a family. And every family that has a lesbian, gay, bisexual, or transgender member is an LGBT family.

That said, when people talk about LGBT families, they usually mean something more specific. If you hear the phrase "LGBT families" in the news, for

The term *LGBT family* can refer to families with LGBT parents or LGBT kids.

example, what's usually meant is parents raising children. That can mean straight parents raising LGBT children, or LGBT parents raising straight children, or any combination of the two.

We know that there are at least 2 million kids with LGBT parents. But whenever we talk about numbers of LGBT people, it is important to keep in mind that not everyone who is LGBT is open about that fact. That's because there's a long history of **discrimination** against LGBT people, and that discrimination continues today. So not everyone who is LGBT is open about it.

Anti-LGBT discrimination has caused, and still causes, a lot of challenges for families. The next chapters will look at the two key aspects of LGBT families—marriage and child raising—and talk about what is being done to make things better.

Text-Dependent Questions

1. What is the difference between *sex* and *gender?*
2. What can the Q stand for in LGBTQ?
3. Roughly, how many kids have LGBT parents?

Research Project

Research how gender roles are portrayed in TV programs, commercials, magazines, and store catalogs. For example, take notes on colors and designs used in girls' clothing versus boys' clothing. What products are aimed at girls and which are targeted at boys, and how were you able to tell? On TV, consider how the actors walk, talk, and behave with each other. Who speaks first; who interrupts more; who is louder, or quieter, or more emotional? Make a chart that shows the different things you've noticed that apply to boys versus girls.

James Obergefell, center, outside the Supreme Court on the morning of the announcement that legalized same-sex marriage in the United States.

Chapter Two

MARRIAGE EQUALITY

On June 26, 2015, the U.S. Supreme Court announced its decision in a case called *Obergefell v. Hodges*. The Court found that states could not prevent gay and lesbian couples from obtaining marriage licenses. Same-sex marriage was already legal in 36 states and in the District of Columbia, but this decision made same-sex marriage legal in all states and U.S. territories.

Words to Understand

apartheid: a political system of racial segregation.

institution: an established organization, custom, or tradition.

invalidate: to negate or overturn.

paupers: historical term for extremely poor people.

polygamy: the practice of one man marrying more than one woman.

secular: not religious.

vetoed: rejected.

It was a long road to get to this point. And even now, not everyone agrees with the Court's decision. To understand where marriage law stands today, it's important to understand a little about the history of marriage as an **institution**.

A BRIEF HISTORY OF MARRIAGE

Marriage has existed in one form or another for at least 4,000 years. But that phrase, "one form or another," is important. Historically, marriages were used to make alliances with other families. It wasn't important that you loved or even liked the person you married. Marriage between cousins has been extremely common throughout history. **Polygamy**, the practice of one man marrying more than one wife, also has a long history. For example, numerous men in the Bible had several wives—even hundreds, in some cases. According to the marriage historian Stephanie Coontz, some families even "married" their children to the spirits of other children who had died!

Governments have been allowing some people to marry, and barring others, for various reasons throughout history. For example, in England in the 1600s, **paupers** could be forbidden from marrying (they often just lived together as husband and wife anyway).

Slaves in the American South could not legally marry. They could marry informally, but their owners could break up their families at any moment. A former slave named Henry "Box" Brown wrote in 1849, "No slave husband has any certainty whatever of being able to retain his wife a single hour; neither has any wife any more certainty of her husband."

There are lots of other examples of governments putting restrictions on who could marry. In Nazi Germany, Jews were not allowed to marry non-Jews. Under the South African system of **apartheid**, people of different races were not allowed to marry. In fact, marriage between races was not fully legal in the United States until 1967 (see sidebar).

The point is, governments have been writing and revising laws about who can marry and who can't for a very long time. Marriage law, much like real-life

The Greek historian Herodotus described a "marriage market" in ancient Babylon, in which eligible young women were auctioned off to older men. This 19th-century painting by Edwin Long is an interpretation of the market Herodotus described.

marriage, is a work in progress. The definition can change depending on the culture of a particular community and the views of the people who live there.

THE RIGHT TO MARRY

On May 18, 1970, Jack Baker and James Michael McConnell attempted to get a marriage license in Minneapolis, Minnesota. Their request for a marriage license was denied, and the two men brought a lawsuit against the state. Their lawsuit traveled through the courts all the way to the Minnesota Supreme Court, where Baker and McConnell lost. The U.S. Supreme Court refused to even consider their case.

Several other couples made attempts at getting same-sex marriage licenses in the 1970s. But at the time, even most LGBT people saw marriage equality as an impossible dream. By the 1980s, activists felt they had far bigger problems to address. Most importantly, the disease AIDS was having a devastating effect on

The Lovings

Mildred and Richard Loving were an average couple in a lot of ways. They had gotten married in June 1958 in Washington, D.C. Then they returned to their home in Virginia to start their family, which would eventually include three children: Donald, Peggy, and Sydney. But one thing made the Lovings stand out: Richard was white, and Mildred was black and Native American.

Mildred and Richard Loving.

In Virginia (and 15 other states), it was illegal for people of different races to marry. The Lovings were arrested in their own bedroom and taken to jail. Their case eventually made it to the Supreme Court, which ruled in 1967 that discrimination in marriage law violated the Fourteenth Amendment to the U.S. Constitution. The case *Loving v. Virginia* is often mentioned in the context of marriage rights for the LGBT community. Many years later, Mildred Loving spoke out in favor of marriage equality for all:

> *Not a day goes by that I don't think of . . . how much it meant to me to have that freedom to marry the person precious to me, even if others thought he was the "wrong kind of person" for me to marry. I believe all Americans, no matter their race, no matter their sex, no matter their sexual orientation, should have that same freedom.*

the LGBT community. The right to a wedding seemed pretty unimportant in face of such a deadly disease.

Except it wasn't unimportant at all. Gay couples had no legal rights. This meant that long-term partners of people with AIDS were often barred from visiting their loved ones in the hospital. Gay couples also couldn't share health insurance. They had no legal rights to inheritance, which meant one partner could easily end up poor or even homeless if the other died. Their children could be taken away. The AIDS crisis underlined the many ways in which LGBT families were experiencing discrimination all the time.

On the positive side, LGBT activists learned a great deal about political organizing. And in the late 1990s, they turned their attention to marriage equality. A major victory came in 2003, when Massachusetts became the first state to allow same-sex couples to marry. (In Europe, the Netherlands and Belgium had already granted this right.) Although the LGBT community celebrated, there was a backlash, too—many states quickly passed laws banning same-sex marriage.

This began a decade of legal back-and-forth on the issue of marriage equality. Lawmakers in California passed a marriage equality law in 2004, but it was **vetoed** twice by then-governor Arnold Schwarzenegger. The opposite

A couple at a marriage equality vigil in California in 2008.

On the evening after the *Obergefell* decision, the White House was lit in rainbow colors to celebrate marriage equality.

occurred in Maine: the governor signed a marriage equality law in 2009, but voters rejected it.

But slowly, attitudes toward same-sex marriage began to change, and soon the laws were changing, too. Marriage equality was legalized in Connecticut in 2008; in Iowa and Vermont in 2009; in New Hampshire and Washington, DC, in 2010; in New York in 2011; and so on.

As activists worked to bring marriage equality to individual states, a number of marriage-related lawsuits were making their way through the U.S. courts. One key decision was *United States v. Windsor* in 2013. This case involved a widow, Edith Windsor, who had been left a large estate by her late wife, Thea Spyer. The two women had been legally married since 2007, but after Spyer died, the Internal Revenue Service (IRS) tried to collect a large portion of the inheritance in taxes. This is something that would not have happened to an opposite-sex couple. Windsor won her case, which was a huge step for the marriage equality movement, because it **invalidated** a law declaring marriage to only involve opposite sex couples.

Then *Obergefell v. Hodges* was announced on June 26, 2015. The decision forced all states to give legal recognition to existing same-sex marriages, and also to begin issuing licenses for new ones. The Court found that the Fourteenth Amendment to the Constitution, which guarantees the right to equal protection under the law, applies to same-sex marriage. In other words, to allow some people to marry but not others is discrimination, and therefore illegal. It was a similar legal argument as that used in the *Loving v. Virginia* case (see sidebar page 24).

As the number of states allowing same-sex marriage has grown, so have the numbers of couples getting married. According to U.S. census figures, there were

Timeline: Marriage Equality around the World

These are countries in which same-sex marriage is legal, listed by year:

2001: The Netherlands

2003: Belgium

2005: Canada, Spain

2006: South Africa

2009: Norway, Sweden

2010: Argentina, Portugal, Iceland

2012: Denmark

2013: Brazil, France, New Zealand, United Kingdom, Uruguay

2014: Finland, Luxembourg

2015: Ireland*, Mexico**, United States

*Ireland is unique because it was the first country to pass marriage equality through a national vote. Other countries achieved marriage equality through either court decisions or laws passed by legislatures.

**Same-sex marriage is allowed in some parts of Mexico and banned in others.

roughly 390,000 same-sex marriages in June 2015. The *Obergefell* decision legalized at least 100,000 more. But only time will tell how many couples will choose to get married in the coming years.

OBJECTIONS TO *OBERGEFELL*

Not everyone agrees that marriage equality is a good thing.

The main argument against same-sex marriage is an objection to LGBT relationships in general. This opinion is usually based in religious faith. For example, some Christians interpret sections of the Bible as declaring same-sex relationships to be sinful. (Not every Christian agrees with this interpretation.) It's important to under-

tand that the *Obergefell* decision only relates to **secular** marriage law. In other words, nothing in the decision says that churches must recognize same-sex couples. No religious group is required to perform same-sex marriages if they don't want to.

Some people are afraid that the institution of marriage is threatened if LGBT couples are allowed to participate. They worry that marriage equality will eventually lead to *anyone* being able to marry *anyone* they want—group marriages, for example, or marriages to children. However, the law defines marriage as a union of *two adults*—not a group (more than two) and not children (not allowed to marry anyone).

A 2015 rally in support of Kim Davis, a county clerk in Kentucky who refused to issue same-sex marriage licenses despite being ordered to do so by a federal court.

As explained in this chapter, marriage has constantly evolved throughout history. The Bible allowed polygamy, but that does not mean we allow it today. Meanwhile, our neighbor, Canada, has had marriage equality for over a decade, and child marriage has not become a problem there.

A final objection is that the Supreme Court shouldn't decide such a huge social change. But about two-thirds of U.S. states already had marriage equality before the decision. So one could debate how major this change truly is. Also, the Court has a long history of weighing in on big social issues, including racial segregation (*Brown v. Board of Education*), the role of prayer in public life (*Engel v. Vitale*), and of course, interracial marriage (*Loving v. Virginia*). The Court has also decided other cases on the issue of gay rights—sometimes in favor (*Romer v. Evans*) and sometimes not (*Boy Scouts of America v. Dale*).

Text-Dependent Questions

1. What is the name of the Supreme Court decision that made same-sex marriage legal across the United States?
2. How did the AIDS crisis affect the marriage equality movement?
3. What is special about marriage equality in Ireland?

Research Project

Research a significant moment in the history of LGBT rights. Explain what happened and why the moment was important. Possible topics to select include:

- the Stonewall Riots in New York City, 1969
- the election of Harvey Milk in San Francisco, 1977
- the founding of the AIDS activist group called ACT UP, 1987
- the Matthew Shepard Act, 2009
- *Obergefell v. Hodges*, 2015

After many studies, there is now widespread agreement that LGBT parents can do their jobs just as well as straight parents.

Chapter Three

RAISING FAMILIES

There have always been LGBT people, and there have always been LGBT families. In the past, LGBT people were less likely to be "out"—meaning they were less likely to be open and honest about their identities or orientations. Lots of kids grew up not even realizing that they had an LGBT parent until much later in life. This still happens today, especially if parents decide to wait to "come out" or transition until their kids are older.

But as old **prejudices** against LGBT people begin to fade, it is becoming more common for parents to be open about themselves. LGBT parents are a visible part of American life.

ARE LGBT PARENTS GOOD PARENTS?

For generations, a **stigma** against LGBT people resulted in many parents losing **custody** of their children. Meanwhile, LGBT people who wanted to adopt were

---

Words to Understand

custody: the right to protect or care for something.

perennial: recurring often.

prejudice: negative attitudes about an entire group.

stigma: the idea that something is wrong or bad.

rejected. The reasoning for all this was that LGBT people would not make good parents. We now know that this was based on prejudice, not fact.

There have been many studies of LGBT parents since the 1980s. In 2015, researchers at Columbia University analyzed 30 years worth of studies on LGBT parenting. Out of 77 different studies that were analyzed, the vast majority concluded that kids raised by LGBT parents have just as good outcomes as kids who were raised by straight parents.

Researchers now largely agree that LGBT parents are just as good at their jobs as straight parents are. The American Academy of Pediatrics (AAP) states that "many studies attest to the normal development of children of same-gender couples." Their report goes on to say that sexual orientation is not a "critical factor" in successful parenting.

Legal Issues

When it comes to LGBT families, the laws are complicated and frequently changing. There are a couple of reasons for this. First, family law—marriage, child custody, adoption, and so on—is written by states. Different states have very different approaches to family law, and also different opinions on LGBT families. What seems normal in California may not be accepted in Mississippi.

A second reason why LGBT family law is changing fast is that marriage equality is new for a lot of states. Lawmakers are still in the process of figuring out what the *Obergefell* decision will mean when it comes to issues like LGBT adoption or same-sex divorce.

Another factor is that many of these issues are resolved in family court, where individual judges have a lot of leeway in making their rulings. That means that the views of a specific judge, whether pro- or anti-LGBT, can have a big impact on the outcome of a case.

Stability and affection matter more in parenting than orientation.

One factor that *is* critical, according to the AAP, is stability. Kids need to feel safe and comfortable. If there is a lot of stress or instability in the home, it's much more likely that the kids will have trouble. This is why the AAP and other kid-focused organizations have strongly supported both marriage equality and LGBT adoption. Marriage and legal adoption are viewed as important ways to increase family stability.

The psychologist Abbie Goldberg, who studies parenting at Clark University, even argues that LGBT parents might be better parents in certain ways. It's pretty rare for LGBT people to become parents by accident—unlike straight couples, LGBT couples usually have to work hard in order to become parents. According to Goldberg, "that translates to greater commitment on average and more involvement."

ADOPTION

Roughly 16,000 LGBT couples are raising more than 22,000 adopted children. That's a much higher rate than straight couples. In fact, LGBT parents are four

Around 16,000 same-sex couples are raising around 22,000 adopted kids.

times more likely to be raising adopted children and six times more likely to be raising foster children.

Sometimes adoption is just a question of one partner adopting the other partner's kids. Legally, it's pretty similar to what happens when a stepparent adopts a child from a previous relationship. But with same-sex couples, the practice is referred to as *second-parent adoption*. Laws about second-parent adoption vary a lot by state. Some states require that the parents be legally married before the adoption can happen. Other states allow unmarried couples to have second-parent adoptions.

To understand how these adoptions work, let's consider Emma from chapter one. Emma is being raised by two moms, Kate and Anne. Kate is Emma's biological mom—that is, she's the woman who actually gave birth to Emma. So Kate is legally Emma's mom. Anne's situation is more complicated. As far as Emma is concerned, both Kate *and* Anne are her moms. But legally, Anne may not have any parental rights. Second-parent adoption makes it possible for Anne and Kate to share custody of Emma. That way, if something bad happens to the family—if Kate gets sick, for example, or if she is suddenly injured—Anne has the legal right to look after Emma.

In other cases, same-sex couples choose adoption as their route to parenthood. (Unattached LGBT people can also adopt sometimes, but again the rules vary by state.) Usually, the adoption process is the same for LGBT couples as it is for straight couples. The wait time is also the same—the Independent Adoption Center says that the process takes about 15 months, regardless of the orientation of the adopting parents.

As with marriage equality, not everyone supports LGBT adoption. For instance, the former U.S. senator and **perennial** presidential candidate Rick Santorum stated repeatedly in 2012 that he believed children would be better off with a parent in jail than they would be with an LGBT parent. This is an extreme view that child-welfare advocates reject. And even Santorum seems to be softening his view: in 2015 he admitted to an interviewer that it was at least theoretically possible for LGBT parents to raise healthy children.

Text-Dependent Questions

1. According to the American Academy of Pediatricians, what is a critical factor in good parenting?
2. What is second-parent adoption?
3. Why does family law vary by state?

Research Project

Find out about family law as it relates to LGBT people in your state and in another state that interests you. (You might start your research at the Lambda Legal website: http://www.lambdalegal.org/in-your-state). Write an essay or make a chart that compares and contrasts the two states.

Members of PFLAG at a Seattle gay pride parade in 2012. PFLAG stands for Parents, Families and Friends of Lesbians and Gays.

Chapter Four

CHALLENGES

The expression *coming out* refers to the process of letting other people know something important about yourself. Originally the term referred to telling people that you are gay. But today people use the term in other situations, too. For instance, if Emma from earlier in the book tells a friend that she has two moms, you might say that Emma came out to her friend as being part of an LGBT family.

Because there is still a lot of discrimination against LGBT people, the process of coming out can be scary. Even if you aren't LGBT but your parents are, it can be frightening to tell people about it. You might worry that you'll be rejected by your friends, or that people will make jokes or say mean things. And unfortunately, that does happen sometimes. Not everyone is ready to accept that someone they know is LGBT or has an LGBT family member.

It's true that some people won't understand. But it's just as true that you can find lots of love and support, if you ask for it. People can surprise you! You might expect that a friend will reject you, only to find that the friend is perfectly fine

Words to Understand

affirming: supportive and encouraging.

project: "PRO-ject"; putting your ideas or feelings on someone else.

tangible: concrete, visible.

with your situation. You also might find the happiness that comes with being loved for who you really are, rather than the stress of pretending to be someone you aren't.

DEALING WITH BAD REACTIONS

That said, it would be wrong to talk about coming out without being honest about the possible bad parts. Some people get angry when they learn that someone they know is LGBT. Some of those reactions are caused by religious faith. If a person believes an interpretation of the Bible that says LGBT lifestyles are bad, then that person might **project** that judgment onto you.

Coming out can be scary if you feel uncertain about how your family will react.

Case Study: Rachel

Rachel is proud of her parents. They are both religious people and are actively involved in their church's ministries, and Rachel grew up with a deep belief in God.

"They taught me that God wants my best," Rachel says. "That God wants me to live with integrity, being true to what the Bible teaches, even when that's hard to do. And I know they live what they teach, because I've seen them."

The most difficult action Rachel has seen her parents take together was the way they handled her father coming to terms with being gay. Rachel says, "When I was 16, my parents sat down with me and told me that my dad was gay. I wasn't really surprised." At the time, having her father move out to live with another man seemed weird. "I was embarrassed to tell some of my friends," Rachel admitted. "And I was mad at him, too, for leaving my mom and me. But I got over it. I got to know Gary, my dad's partner. He's a nice guy, and I can see how happy he and my dad are together."

"Maybe my life would have been easier in some ways if my father hadn't been gay—but by his coming out when he did, he forced me to think about things that are important. He helped me realize what I truly value in life and what I want to do. I want to do something to help change the world so that gay people have the same rights and respect as everybody else."

Adapted from *Gay and Lesbian Parents* by Julianna Fields (Mason Crest, 2010).

Sometimes people react badly because they are afraid. Maybe they worry that you won't be the same person anymore. Or they might feel upset that you kept a secret—that they didn't know you as well as they thought. Parents worry that their LGBT child's life will be harder than a straight child's life. Sometimes people just feel threatened by people who are different. They want everyone to be the same as them because it makes life simpler.

Try to remember that these bad reactions say more about the other person than they do about you. For instance, not all Christians interpret the Bible in the same way. So if someone says LGBT people are bad because of the Bible, remember that's *their* interpretation of the Bible. Lots of other Christians interpret it differently.

DISCRIMINATION AND BULLYING

Unfortunately, negative feelings about LGBT people can translate into negative actions. People make jokes or say mean things. Sometimes LGBT people are abused or hurt. Some parents reject their LGBT kids—as many as 40 percent of homeless kids are LGBT. So while coming out can be a wonderful and **affirming** process, it does have risks. Experts advise kids to think carefully about their safety before coming out to people who might not be supportive. "Coming out is not the solution to [all] your problems," says the advice columnist Dan Savage. "Coming out is often the beginning of new problems."

The LGBT community experiences many types of discrimination, including in jobs, housing, health care, and access to government services. Fewer than one-third of U.S. states have outlawed discrimination against people based on sexual orientation. Even fewer have outlawed discrimination based on gender identity (such as being transgender).

Discrimination has direct impacts on LGBT families. Some parents have trouble finding jobs, or they may lose the jobs they have. Transgender people are four times more likely to live in poverty than other people, and if they have children, their children are poor, too. Kids of LGBT families might be denied health insurance or refused access to government aid, because their parents might not have legal custody. LGBT couples have had problems with taxes, retirement benefits, and inheritance. They are at greater risk of losing custody of their children,

An estimated 40 percent of homeless teens are LGBT kids who were forced out of their homes.

simply because they are LGBT. Women and people of color who are also LGBT tend to suffer the most, since they experience discrimination due to both their race or gender *and* their orientation.

Then there are the less **tangible**, but still damaging, forms of discrimination. A group called the Gay, Lesbian & Straight Education Network (GLSEN) conducted a nationwide survey in 2013 and found that 55 percent of LGBT students felt unsafe at school. The survey found a huge range of outcomes, depending on where the students lived: in South Carolina, Missouri, Maine, and Indiana, more than 80 percent of students reported verbal harassment; the lowest rate was in Massachusetts, but the rate was still 58 percent. In Tennessee, 48 percent of LGBT students in the survey reported physical harassment (pushing or shoving), while in Maryland that number was 20 percent. Alabama had the highest rates of physical assault (hitting, kicking, and so on), at 28 percent, and Connecticut had the lowest, at 5 percent.

IT GETS BETTER

Of course, even 5 percent of LGBT students being physically assaulted is far too many. Bullying doesn't just hurt; it also results in more school absences and lower achievement. It makes LGBT kids feel like they are not an accepted part of their community. Groups like GLSEN and many others are working with schools to create anti-bullying programs and to help teach students that they have nothing to fear from LGBT kids or their parents.

The LGBT community has seen a remarkable increase in acceptance during the past generation. Not long ago, few people believed that marriage equality

A 2014 gay pride parade in the seemingly unlikely location of Istanbul, Turkey. Even if you sometimes feel like nobody understands you, trust that there are people out there who will. Don't give up!

was possible; now it is the law of not only the United States, but also of increasing numbers of other countries. There is still a lot of work to be done to make LGBT families safer and more equal. But we have good reason to hope that as marriage equality takes hold, we will start to see even more positive change.

Text-Dependent Questions

1. What are some of the possible positive aspects of coming out? What are some of the possible negative aspects?
2. What percentage of LGBT kids feel unsafe in school?
3. What types of discrimination do LGBT families experience?

Research Project

Find out what resources your school and community offer to LGBT people. (You can start your search with the websites listed at the back of this book.) Resources can include places like an LGBT center at a local college, a community "rainbow" or "pride" group, and support groups that meet in your area. Also include anti-bullying programs and any Gay-Straight Alliance groups your school might have. Write up a directory of resources that other students can use.

FURTHER READING

Books

Belge, Kathy and Marke Bieschke. *Queer: The Ultimate LGBT Guide for Teens*. San Francisco, CA: Zest Books, 2011.

Dawson, James. *This Book is Gay*. Naperville, IL: Sourcebooks, 2015.

Huegel, Kelly. *GLBTQ: The Survival Guide for Gay, Lesbian, Bisexual, Transgender, and Questioning Teens*. Minneapolis, MN: Free Spirit Publishing, 2011.

Shelton, Michael. *Family Pride: What LGBT Families Should Know about Navigating Home, School, and Safety in Their Neighborhoods*. Boston, MA: Beacon Press, 2013.

Online

Everyone is Gay. http://www.everyoneisgay.com.

Gay, Lesbian & Straight Education Network. http://www.glsen.org/.

GLAAD. http://www.glaad.org.

GLAAD. "An Ally's Guide to Terminology: Talking about LGBT People and Equality." http://www.glaad.org/sites/default/files/allys-guide-to-terminology_1.pdf.

It Gets Better Project. http://www.itgetsbetter.org.

Get Help Now

The Trevor Project

A 24/7 crisis hotline for LGBT people from 13 to 24 years old.

1-866-4-U-TREVOR   http://www.thetrevorproject.org/

SERIES GLOSSARY

agencies: departments of a government with responsibilities for specific programs.

anxiety: a feeling of worry or nervousness.

biological parents: the woman and man who create a child; they may or not raise it.

caregiving: helping someone with their daily activities.

cognitive: having to do with thinking or understanding.

consensus: agreement among a particular group of people.

custody: legal guardianship of a child.

demographers: people who study information about people and communities.

depression: severe sadness or unhappiness that does not go away easily.

discrimination: singling out a group for unfair treatment.

disparity: a noticeable difference between two things.

diverse: having variety; for example, "ethnically diverse" means a group of people of many different ethnicities.

ethnicity: a group that has a shared cultural heritage.

extended family: the kind of family that includes members beyond just parents and children, such as aunts, uncles, cousins, and so on.

foster care: raising a child (usually temporarily) that is not adopted or biologically yours.

heir: someone who receives another person's wealth and social position after the other person dies.

homogenous: a group of things that are the same.

ideology: a set of ideas and ways of seeing the world.

incarceration: being confined in prison or jail.

inclusive: accepting of everyone.

informally: not official or legal.

institution: an established organization, custom, or tradition.

kinship: family relations.

neglect: not caring for something correctly.

patriarchal: a system that is run by men and fathers.

prejudice: beliefs about a person or group based only on simplified and often mistaken ideas.

prevalence: how common a particular trait is in a group of people.

psychological: having to do with the mind.

quantify: to count or measure objectively.

restrictions: limits on what someone can do.

reunification: putting something back together.

secular: nonreligious.

security: being free from danger.

social worker: a person whose job is to help families or children deal with particular problems.

socioeconomic: relating to both social factors (such as race and ethnicity) as well as financial factors (such as class).

sociologists: people who study human society and how it operates.

spectrum: range.

stability: the sense that things will stay the same.

stereotype: a simplified idea about a type of person that is not connected to actual individuals.

stigma: a judgment that something is bad or shameful.

stressor: a situation or event that causes upset (stress).

traumatic: something that's very disturbing and causes long-term damage to a person.

variable: something that can change.

INDEX

Page numbers in *italics* refer to photographs or tables.

ABOUT THE AUTHOR

H. W. Poole is a writer and editor of books for young people, including the 13-volume set, *Mental Illnesses and Disorders: Awareness and Understanding* (Mason Crest). She created the *Horrors of History* series (Charlesbridge) and the *Ecosystems* series (Facts On File). She has also been responsible for many critically acclaimed reference books, including *Political Handbook of the World* (CQ Press) and the *Encyclopedia of Terrorism* (SAGE). She was coauthor and editor of *The History of the Internet* (ABC-CLIO), which won the 2000 American Library Association RUSA award.

PHOTO CREDITS